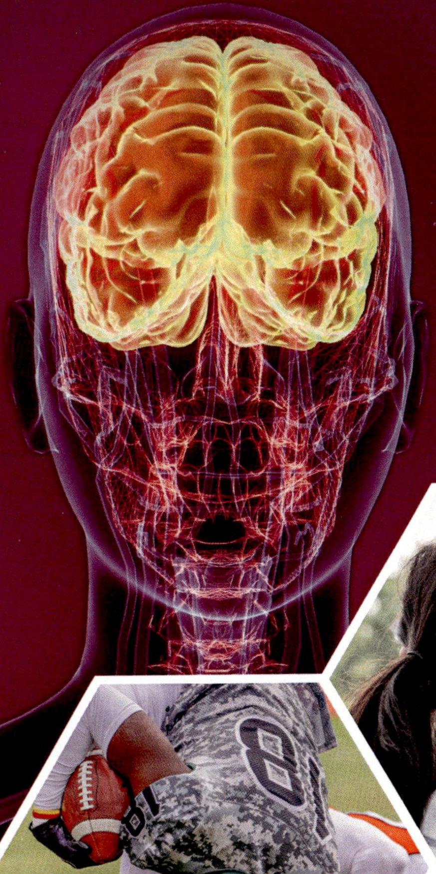

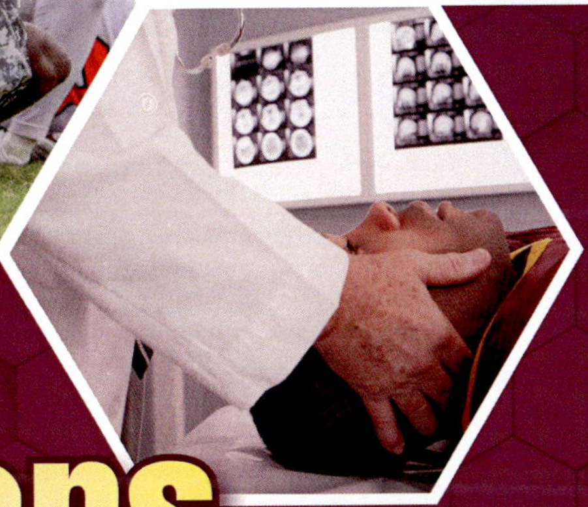

India James

SPORTS INJURIES

Concussions

A Crabtree Forest Book

Crabtree Publishing

crabtreebooks.com

School-to-Home Support for Caregivers and Teachers

This appealing book is designed to teach students about core subject areas. Students will build upon what they already know about the subject and engage in topics that they want to learn more about. Here are a few guiding questions to help readers build comprehension skills. Possible answers appear here in red.

Before Reading:

- What do I know about concussions?
  - *I know that concussions are a head injury*
  - *I know that concussions happen when you hit your head*
- What do I want to learn about this topic?
  - *I want to know about brain anatomy*
  - *I want to know how to prevent concussions*

During Reading:

- I'm curious to know...
  - *I'm curious to know what I may feel like after a concussion*
  - *I'm curious to know what might happen at a doctor's office after a concussion*
- How is this like something I already know?
  - *I know that concussions often happen in contact sports*
  - *I know that concussions happen to any athlete, from kids to professionals*

After Reading:

- What was the author trying to teach me?
  - *The author was trying to teach me that there are many types of concussions*
  - *The author was trying to teach me that the symptoms of concussions may last a long time*
- How did the photographs and captions help me understand more?
  - *The drawing of brain anatomy helped me understand the protective layers around the brain*
  - *The chart of the NFL Concussion Game Day Checklist helped me understand how professionals evaluate concussions*

Table of Contents

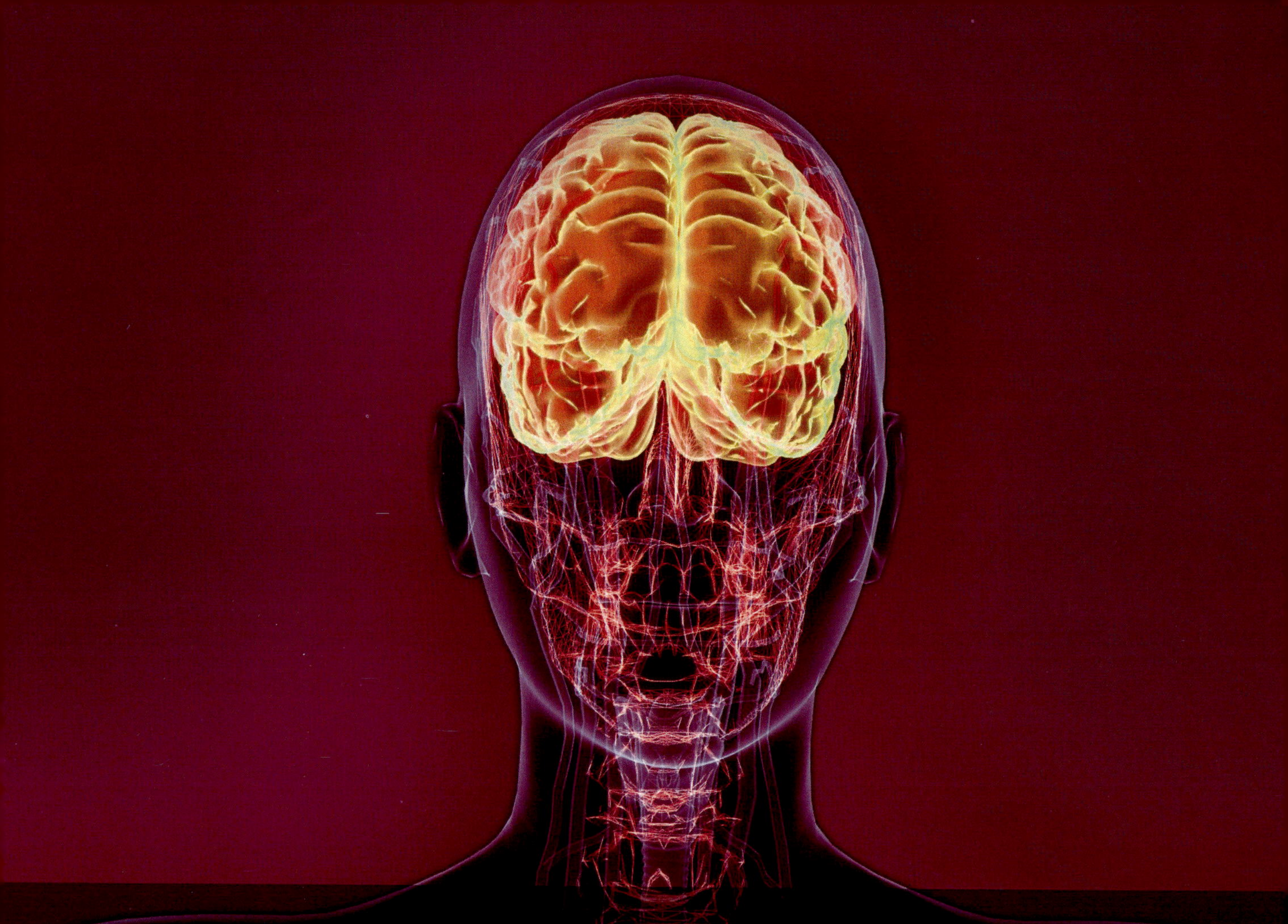

Chapter 1: What are concussions?

The goalie lunges forward toward the ball, protecting her goal. Then, out of nowhere, another player's knee collides with the side of her head. The two players collapse on the field. They both stand up, but when the goalie looks around, everything is blurry. She can't walk in a straight line. What happened?

A football ball sails 18 yards down the field. The tight end reaches up, catches it, but he is immediately tackled and thrown to the ground. As the players around him get to his feet, the tight end stays down. He clutches his head. Many minutes later, he can't even sit up. Eventually, he's taken off the field in a stretcher. What happened?

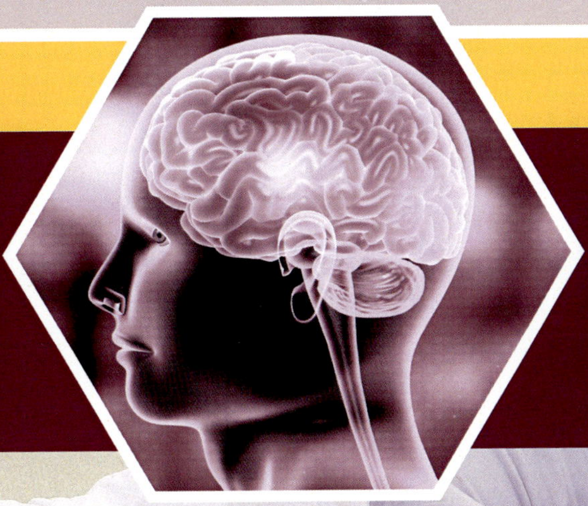

Concussions

Both of these athletes had concussions. A concussion is a mild **traumatic** brain injury that changes the way the brain works. Most people can recover from concussions, but being repeatedly injured with concussions may lead to more severe brain injury.

Concussions are common sports injuries, but they often happen outside of sports, too. Both sports concussions and concussions from other events result in more than one million emergency room (ER) visits a year!

The Centers for Disease Control and Prevention (CDC) in the United States has started keeping track of how many athletes are injured with concussions each year. The scientists there estimate that 2 in every 10 high school athletes who play a contact sport will have a concussion in any year.

Concussions are a common injury in contact sports. Lacrosse, football, hockey, and soccer have the highest numbers of concussions per player in both youth and adult athletes. These contact sports involve many tackles and collisions. However, you can also get a concussion without being tackled. In soccer, **heading** the ball is one way that players can get a concussion without any contact from another player.

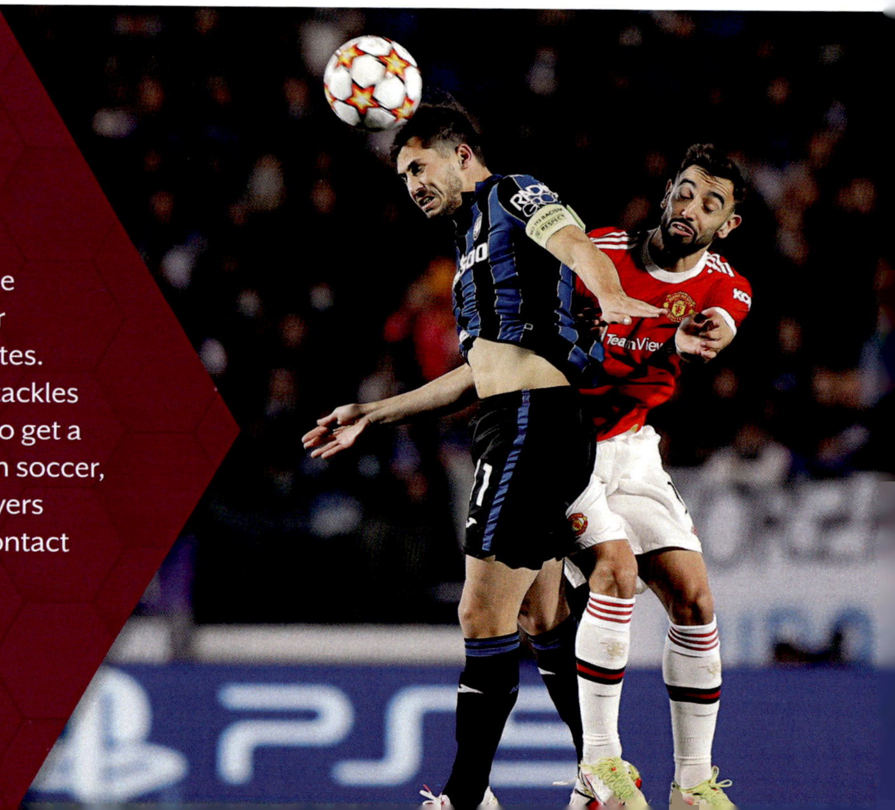

There's a risk of concussions in any sport where a player's head is hit, but there are ways to help prevent this brain injury. Doctors and scientists who study the brain have come up with treatment plans after a concussion occurs. You can reduce the risk of a concussion by understanding how this injury occurs.

Chapter 2: Anatomy

Anatomy describes body parts and how they work together. Understanding how injuries happen starts with knowing the way your body's **tissue**, bones, and fluids function.

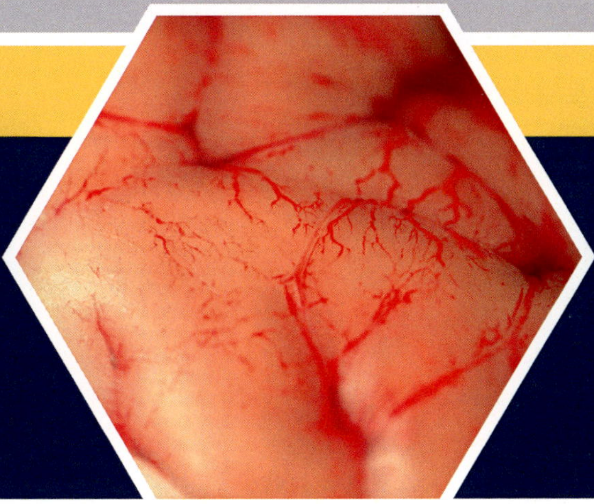

Brain tissue

Your brain controls every part of your body. It is what makes you, you. Your brain is made of grey and white tissue. The cells in your brain's grey tissue send messages to other cells that are nearby. The **cells** in your brain's white tissue send messages to parts of your brain and **spinal cord** that are farther away.

Concussions have been around for a long time! The oldest writing that talks about concussions is from a Persian physician named Rhazes. He identified some of the symptoms of the injury in the 10th century CE.

Bones and Joints

Your brain's soft tissue is protected by the hard **cranial bones** of your **skull**. You have eight cranial bones:

- Frontal bone
- Two parietal bones
- Occipital bone
- Two temporal bones
- Sphenoid bone
- Ethmoid **bone**

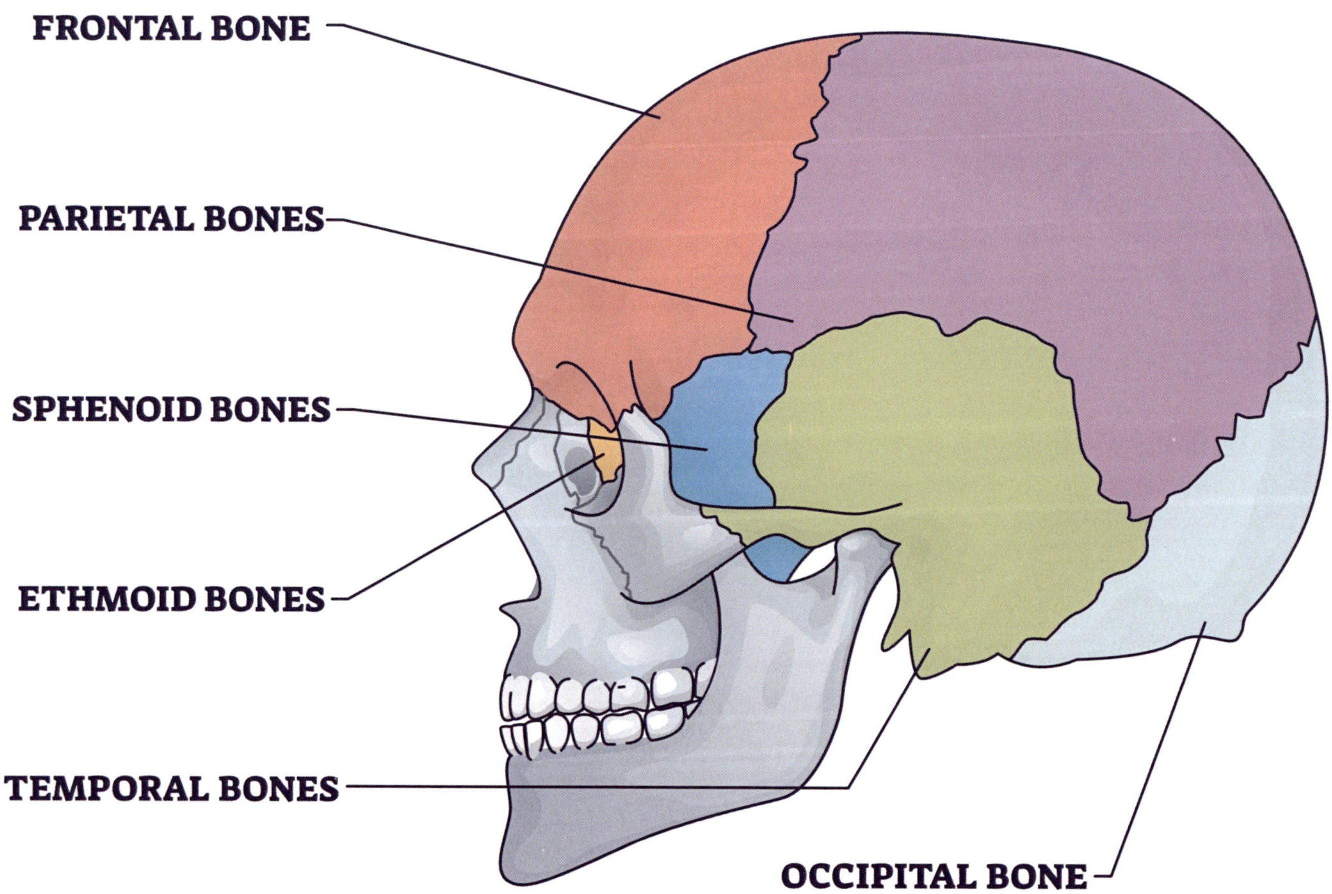

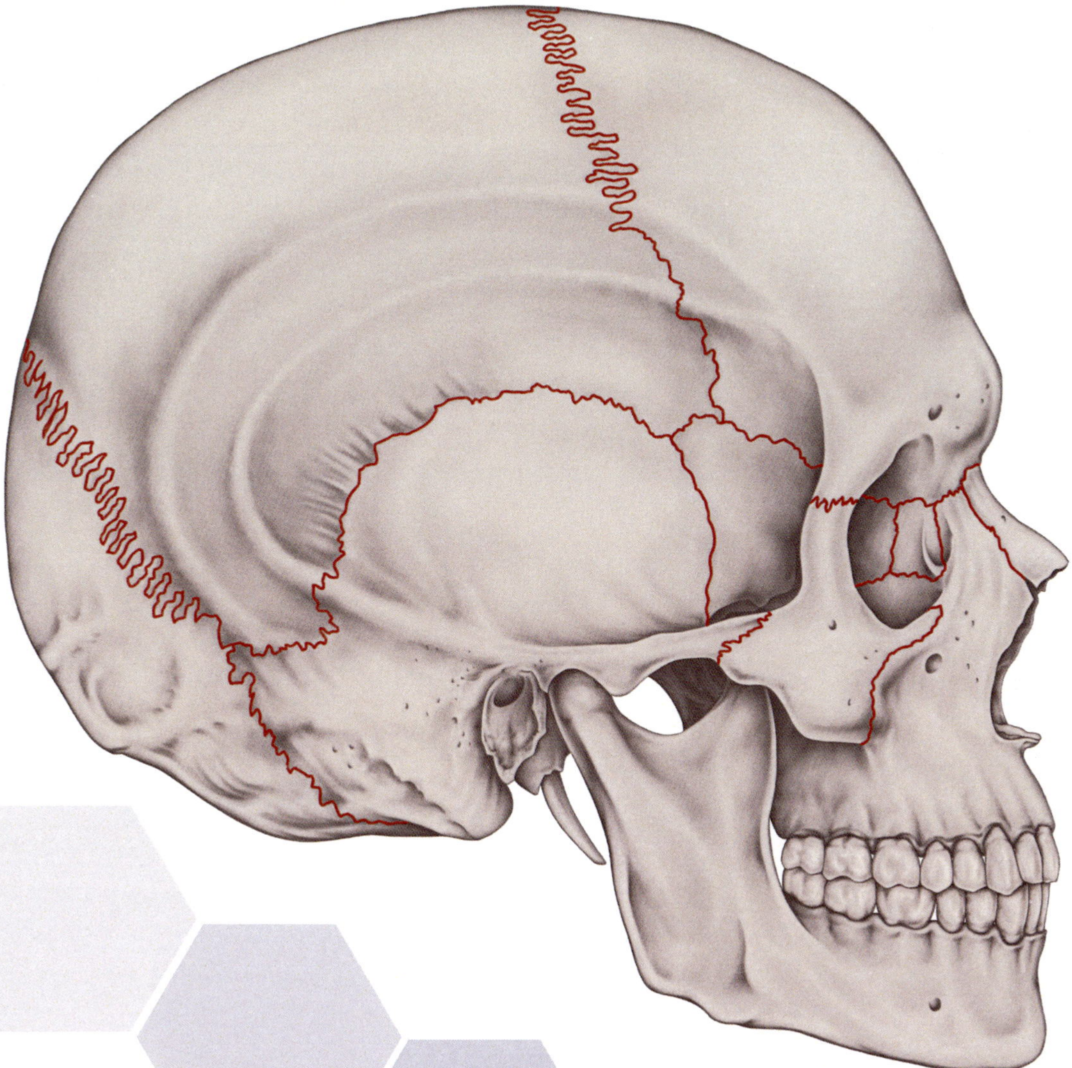

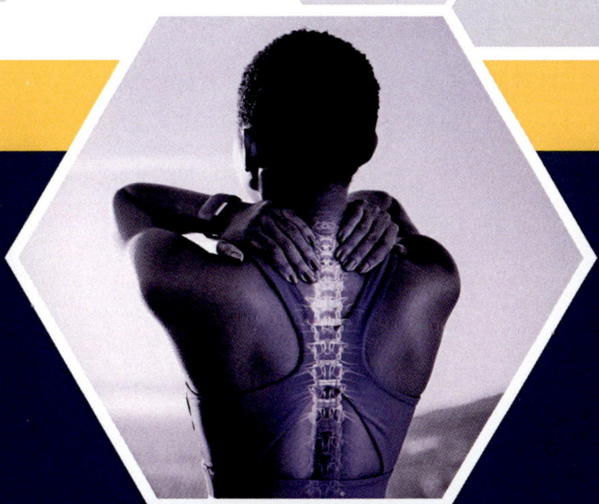

Joints

The place where two or more bones come together is called a **joint**. Some joints in your body, such as your knees, shoulders, and hips, move a lot. Other joints, such as the bones of your spine, move just a little bit. Some joints, such as the cranial bones of your skull, don't move at all. These are called immoveable joints. The part of your skull that protects your brain feels solid because of these immoveable joints.

Meninges

It's important to protect your brain **tissue,** and this job falls to more than just your cranial bones. Three structures between your skull and your brain tissue act like a cushion to help keep your brain tissue safe. These three layers together are called the **meninges.** The three layers are

- **Dura matter**
- **Arachnoid**
- **Pia matter**

Pia mater and dura mater get their names from words in Latin. Pia matter means "soft mother" or "tender mother," and dura matter means "hard mother."

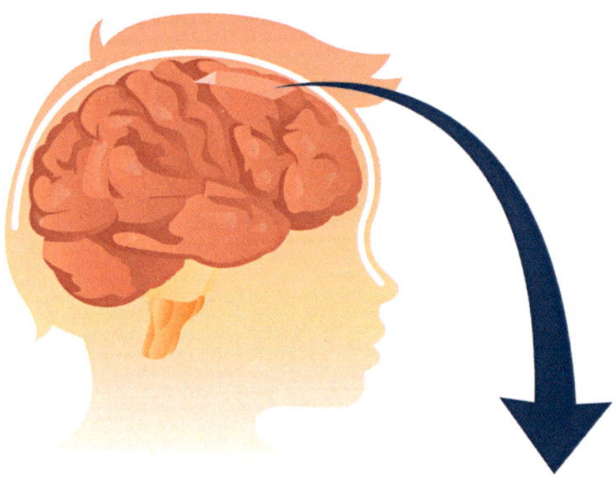

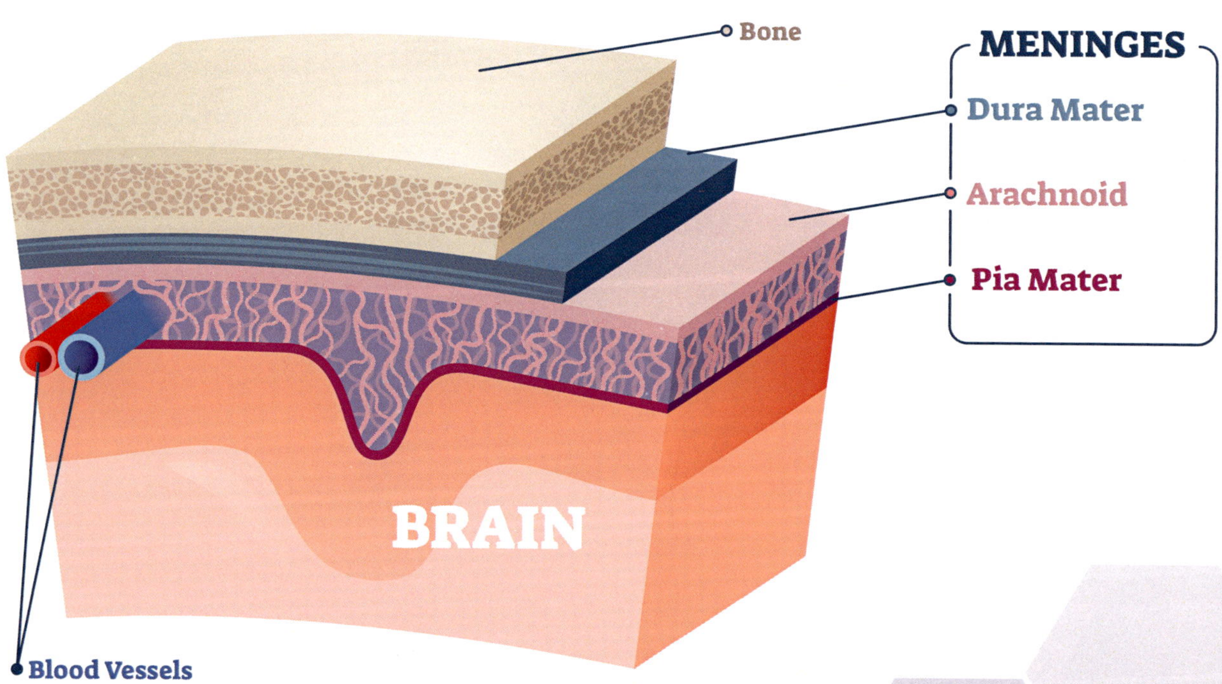

The dura matter is closest to your cranial bones. It is a thick, strong membrane made up of two different layers of tissue.

The arachnoid is the middle layer. It looks like a spiderweb, which is what gives this structure its name.

The pia matter is the layer closest to your brain tissue. It acts like shrink wrap to help connect blood vessels to your brain tissue.

In between the arachnoid and the pia matter, there's one other material helping to protect your brain. The space between these two structures is filled with **cerebrospinal fluid.** This fluid is another cushion between your brain tissue and cranial bones.

Cerebrospinal fluid

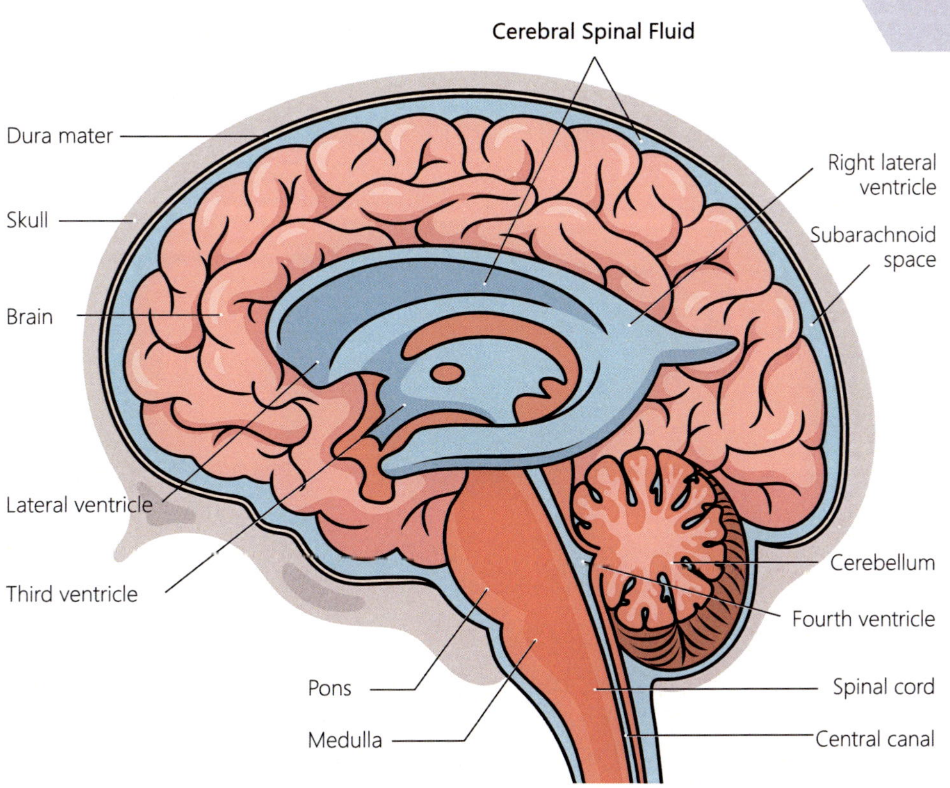

Chapter 3: Causes of injury

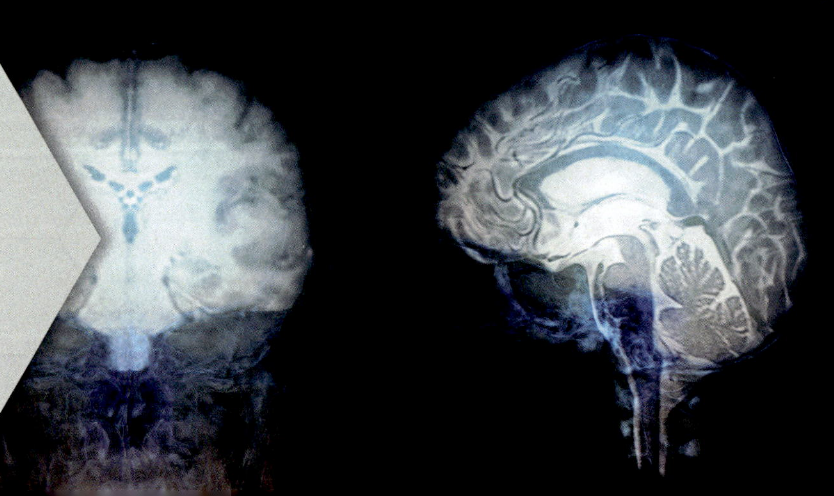

Inside your skull, there's some room for your brain tissue to move around. This movement is usually protected by the meninges and the cerebrospinal fluid. But sometimes, your brain tissue can move too fast or too hard.

When your brain tissue moves too hard or too fast, the meninges and cerebrospinal fluid aren't enough of a cushion. Your brain tissue can hit the hard bones of your skull and get hurt. This injury is called a concussion.

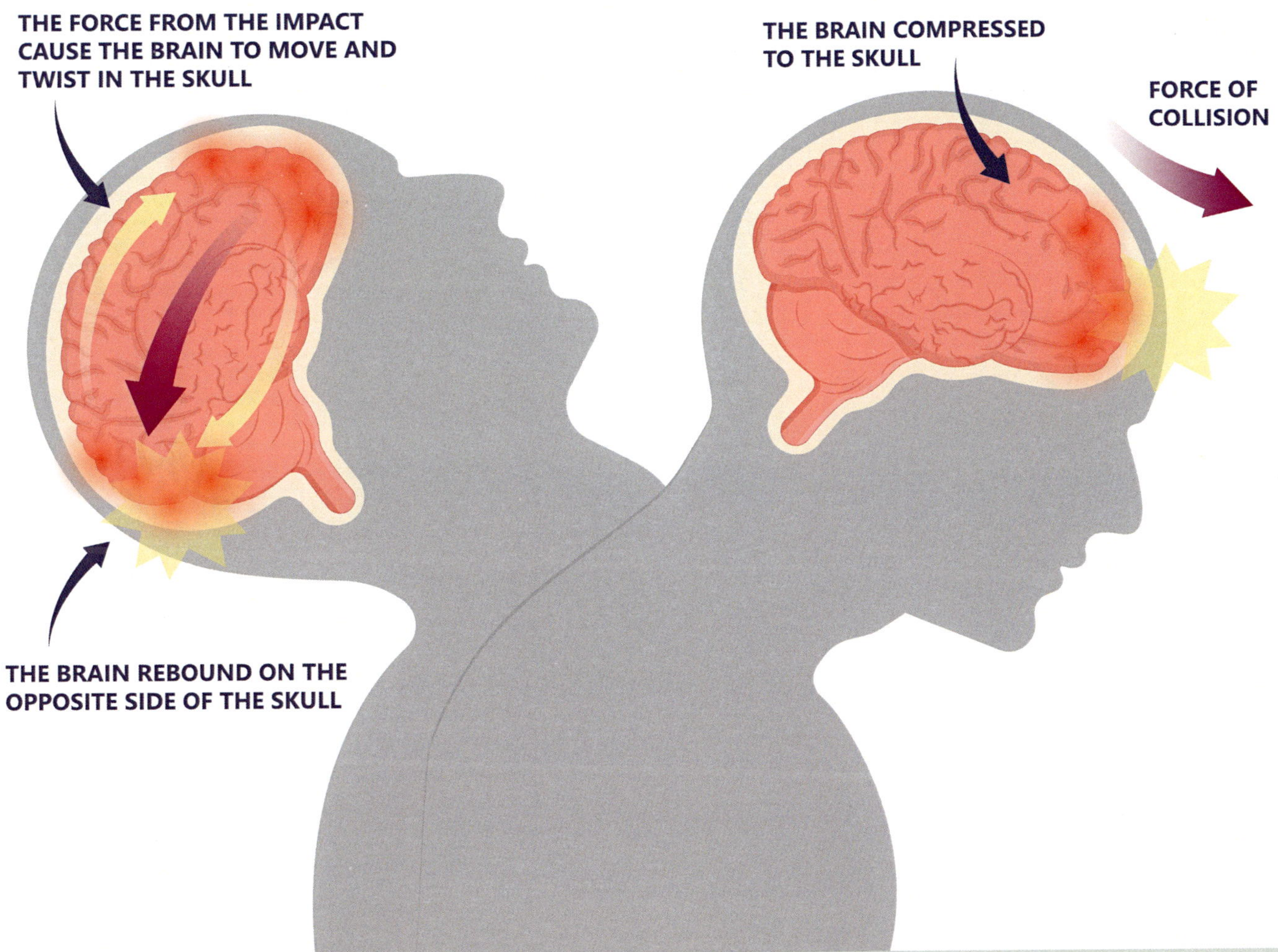

One of the most common causes of a concussion is when your head hits something. For an athlete, this can be when your head hits the ground, like during a tackle. Or, it can be when a piece of equipment like a ball, bat, or stick makes contact with your head. It can even be when your head hits another player.

Whiplash

Concussions don't have to happen because of a direct hit. **Whiplash** is one way that your brain can be injured without a hit. Whiplash is when your head is suddenly thrust forward or backward while rotating on the neck. The sudden movement can make your brain tissue hit the cranial bones, just like a hit to the head. However, concussions from whiplash aren't very common in sports. These types of concussions are more often seen during car crashes.

Chapter 4: Symptoms and Types of Concussions

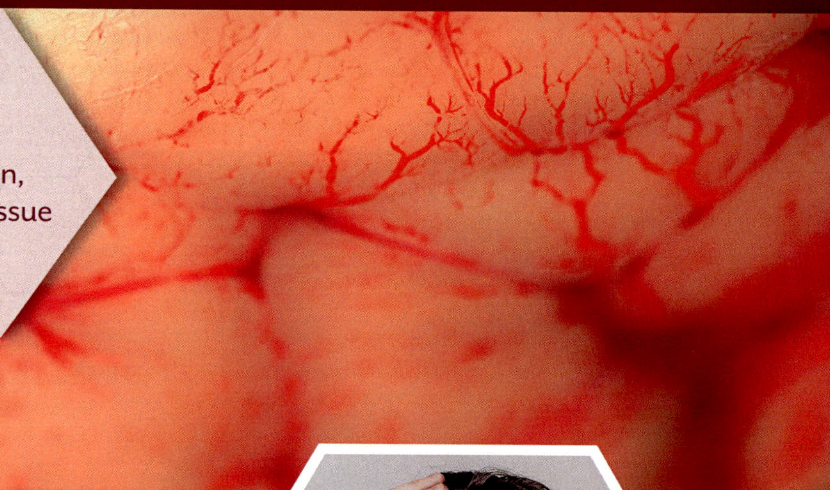

Your brain tissue is injured when it hits the cranial bones. But you may have different symptoms of a concussion, depending on what part of your brain tissue was hurt.

Anxiety-Mood

An anxiety-mood concussion is when your injury makes it hard for your brain to control your emotions. If you have this type of a concussion, you may begin to feel nervous or anxious. You might become depressed or have trouble controlling anger. These are all symptoms of the anxiety-mood type of concussion.

Cognitive

Sometimes after a concussion, you may have trouble focusing your attention or recalling things you should remember. When you have these symptoms, you have a cognitive type of concussion.

Headache

This type concussion is also called a migraine type. If you have bad headaches after an injury, you have this type of concussion.

Ocular-motor

Anytime after you hit your head and then have trouble seeing, you have an ocular-motor type of concussion. You might not be able to read words, or you might have blurred or double vision.

Vestibular

Dizziness, nausea, and **vertigo** are all symptoms of a vestibular type of concussion.

These five types of concussions help describe what type of injury you might have. But you might also have symptoms from more than one type of concussion. You might even find that your type of concussion changes as you recover.

Scientists and doctors who study concussions have found that some types are more likely to occur together than other types. Cognitive and ocular-motor concussions are the most common.

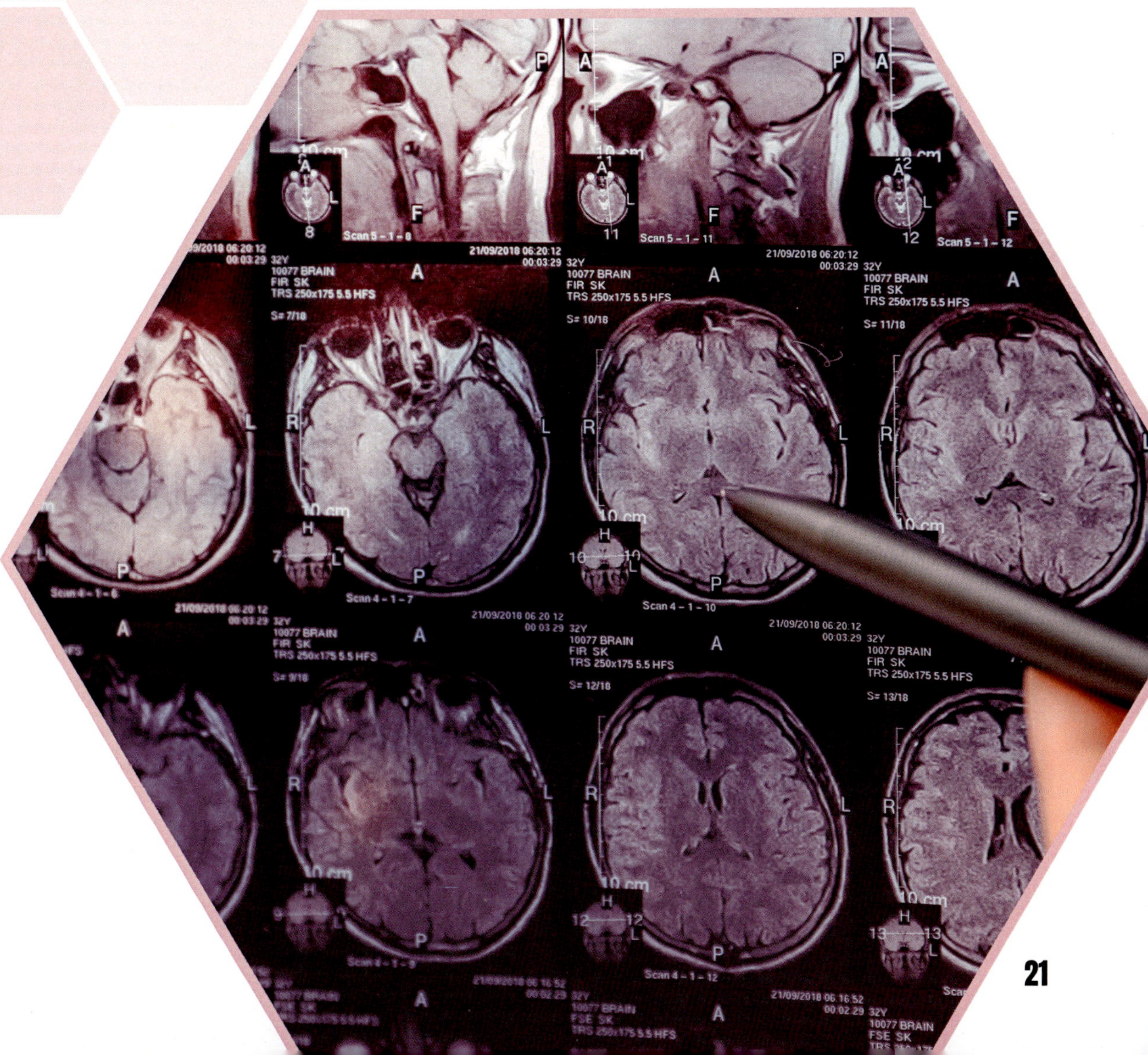

Concussion Severity

Concussions can range from mild to severe injuries. Doctors and medical professionals have developed a grading system to help identify how badly you're hurt. They use this grading system to recommend treatment.

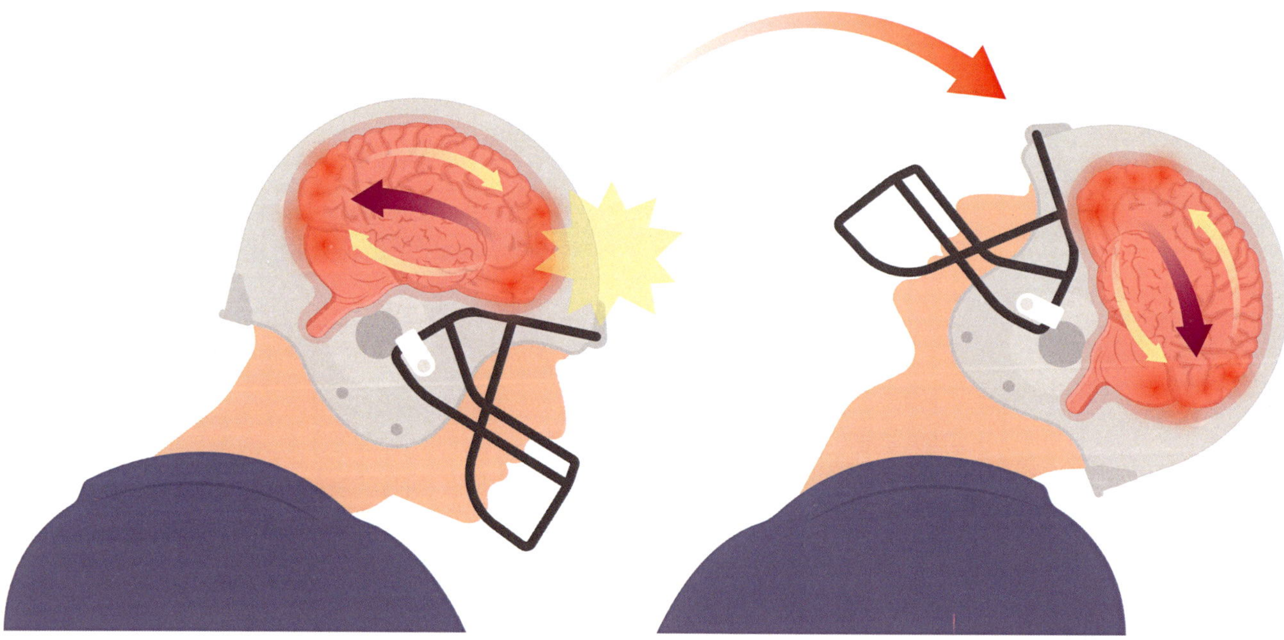

Grade 1 concussions mean that you were injured without losing consciousness. If you have a Grade 1 concussion, it also means that you may have had trouble with your memory for less than 30 minutes.

Grade 2 concussions mean that you were injured and unconscious for less than 5 minutes. If you have a Grade 2 concussion, it also means that you may have had trouble remembering things for between 30 minutes and 24 hours after your injury.

Grade 3 concussions mean that you were injured and unconscious for more than 5 minutes and have had trouble with your memory for more than a day after injury.

Chapter 5: Diagnosis

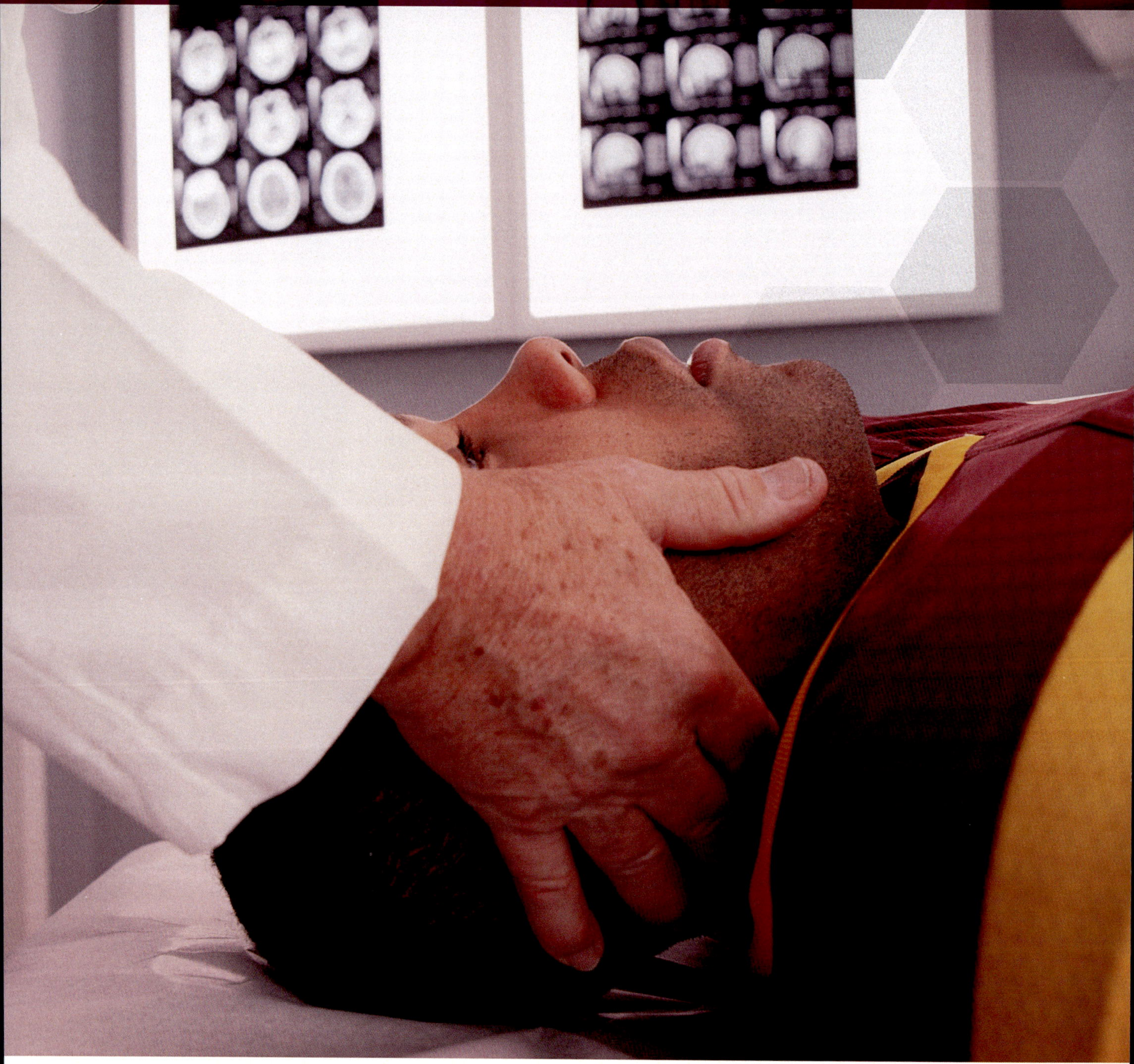

Immediately after injury

It's important to be examined quickly after your head is hit to see if you've had a concussion. It's also important to be examined if you feel any symptoms of a concussion The faster you're treated, the less likely your concussion is to get worse.

Coaches and athletic trainers are with athletes at every practice and game, and these leaders are trained to recognize symptoms of a concussion. Many sports leagues have created guidelines to help coaches and trainers to identify concussions quickly.

Concussions are common in football, and the National Football League (NFL) has developed a Concussion Game Day Checklist.

The first point on the checklist to take a player off the field immediately after an impact or when he first starts having symptoms of a concussion. The checklist then tells the coaches and trainers to use video to review the play and look at the impact. Meanwhile, doctors and trainers examine the player for trouble with his memory and nausea. These medical professionals will also ask the player some simple questions. If the player can't answer the questions or has any physical symptoms, then the NFL rules say that he is not allowed to return to the game or practice.

NFL CONCUSSION GAME DAY CHECKLIST

Player receives impact to the head **AND** Player exhibits or reports symptoms or signs suggestive of a concussion or stinger **OR** ATC, booth ATC, team physician, NFL official, teammate or UNC initiates protocol

Player is immediately removed to sideline or stabilized on field, as needed.

SIDELINE SURVEY

Removed helmet. Team Physician and UNC perform **sideline survey**:

- No-Go
- History of Event
- Concussion Signs/Symptoms
- Maddock's Questions
- Video Review
- Focused Neurological Exam:
  - Cervical Spine Exam (including range of motion-pain)
  - Evaluation of Speech
  - Observation of Gait
  - Eye Movement and Pupillary Exam

If normal sideline survey and "benign" video, player may **RETURN TO PLAY**.

NO-GO

- LOC
- Confusion
- Amnesia

If observed at any point, **NO RETURN TO PLAY**

If any elements are positive, inconclusive or suspicious of concussion, player is escorted to locker room.

LOCKER ROOM EXAM

Team Physician/ UNC/ ATC ***OR***

Team Physician/ UNC perform **locker room exam**:

- Complete NFL SCAT
- Complete Neurological Exam

If normal assessment, player may **RETURN TO PLAY**.

If abnormal, NO RETURN TO PLAY:

- Player stays in locker room
- Periodic evaluation by medical team
- Follow-up neurological exam

The NFL developed their Concussion Protocol in 2011. Doctors, scientists, coaches, and trainers review it every year to make sure it is using the most current medical advice.

Many other sports follow routines similar to the NFL's. The National Women's Soccer League (NWSL), the National Basketball Association (NBA), and the Women's National Basketball League (WNBA) have guidelines that require a player to be removed from the game or practice if they have a concussion. Each of these sports leagues, and many others, recognize that concussions are dangerous injuries.

Complete Exam

Whether you're a youth athlete or a professional athlete, an exam for a concussion follows the same procedure. After you've been removed from play or practice, an evaluation will take place in a quiet environment. Different types of concussions have different symptoms, and doctors will examine for each type.

During your exam, the doctor will ask you to perform physical tasks. One of these might be a balance test. During the balance test, the doctor may tell you to stand in three different positions:

- with both feet shoulder-width apart
- with one foot in front of the other
- on just one leg

You will try to hold these positions for 20 seconds each.

The doctor will also ask you to perform mental tasks. You might need to read numbers off of a card, or you might be asked to memorize a series of words and say them back to the doctor. The doctor may ask you to say the months of the year in reverse order. All of these tasks help the doctor understand how your brain is functioning.

Imaging

There's no way to take a picture of your brain to determine if you have a concussion. However, doctors may order **Magnetic Resonance Imaging** (MRI) or **X-ray** images to help with their diagnosis. A CT scan (computerized tomography) is a series of X-rays that the doctor may order as well. Doctors may want these images to see if there is another injury, like a bone fracture.

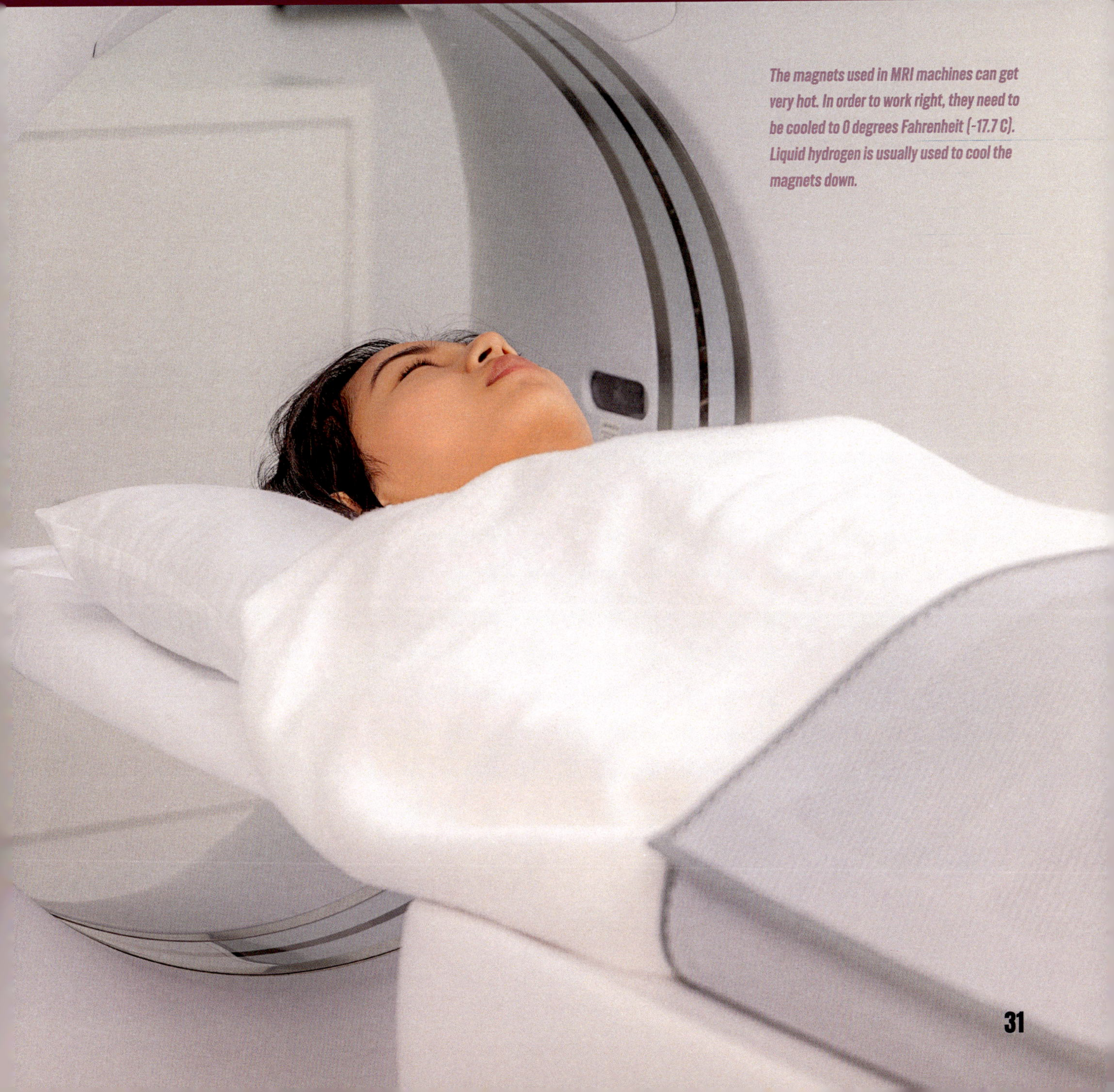

The magnets used in MRI machines can get very hot. In order to work right, they need to be cooled to 0 degrees Fahrenheit (-17.7 C). Liquid hydrogen is usually used to cool the magnets down.

Chapter 6: Treatment

The most important part of treatment for a concussion is to rest. You will be able to recover from most concussions, but returning to play too quickly could turn a mild injury into a severe one.

In many cases, you'll be able to go home from the exam right away. In severe cases, a doctor may want you to stay overnight in a hospital for observation. The doctor will decide this based on your symptoms.

If you're diagnosed with a concussion, you'll be told to rest from any activity that requires concentration. Both physical and mental activities can put demands on your brain, and your brain needs time to heal after injury. Your doctor may tell you to stay away from screens such as computers, TV, and video games as well as books, schoolwork, and texting.

Chapter 7: Recovery

Recovering from a concussion takes time. After a few days of rest, the doctor may tell you to start increasing activity. This might include jogging or riding a stationary bike. You should only do the activities that the doctor says is okay. It's important not to do anything where you might hit your head again.

As you recover and increase your activity, your doctor will also give you instructions on how to return to other parts of normal life as well. Your doctor might tell you to only go to school for a few hours at a time at first. You and your doctor will discuss how to increase your activity back to normal.

X-rays were discovered by accident. Wilhelm Roentgen, a professor of physics, was doing an experiment in 1895 when he found that a mysterious green light could pass through heavy black paper. He soon found that this light could take pictures of bones.

Post-Concussion Syndrome

In most cases, concussions will heal on their own. You should go back to feeling normal within a few days or weeks. However, sometimes symptoms of a concussion last for a long time. These symptoms can include dizziness, headaches, trouble concentrating or remembering things, or anxiety and depression. If this happens, you might have post-concussion syndrome.

Treatment for post-concussion syndrome depends on the symptoms. A doctor will be able to help you find additional treatment. Specialized doctors may be able to prescribe medicine for headaches or dizziness. You may need speech or occupational therapy for problems talking or with **motor skills.** Counseling can be useful for anxiety and depression.

Chronic traumatic encephalopathy

Chronic traumatic encephalopathy (CTE) is a rare brain disorder that seems to come from repeated hits to the head or repeated concussions. In CTE, brain cells die over time and cause memory and behavior problems such as

- problems planning and carrying out tasks
- aggression
- depression
- trouble walking and talking
- substance misuse

Doctors and scientists don't completely understand this disorder. They've found signs of CTE in the brains of former football players and other people who have taken many hits to head. However, they don't know how many concussions or hits a person needs in order to develop CTE.

Symptoms of CTE don't develop right away. An athlete may not show any symptoms for 20 or 30 years. That makes it hard to connect the cause of the injury to symptoms.

CTE seems to develop from many injuries, not a single concussion. But this is a serious disorder. It's important to take steps to protect your brain from any concussions.

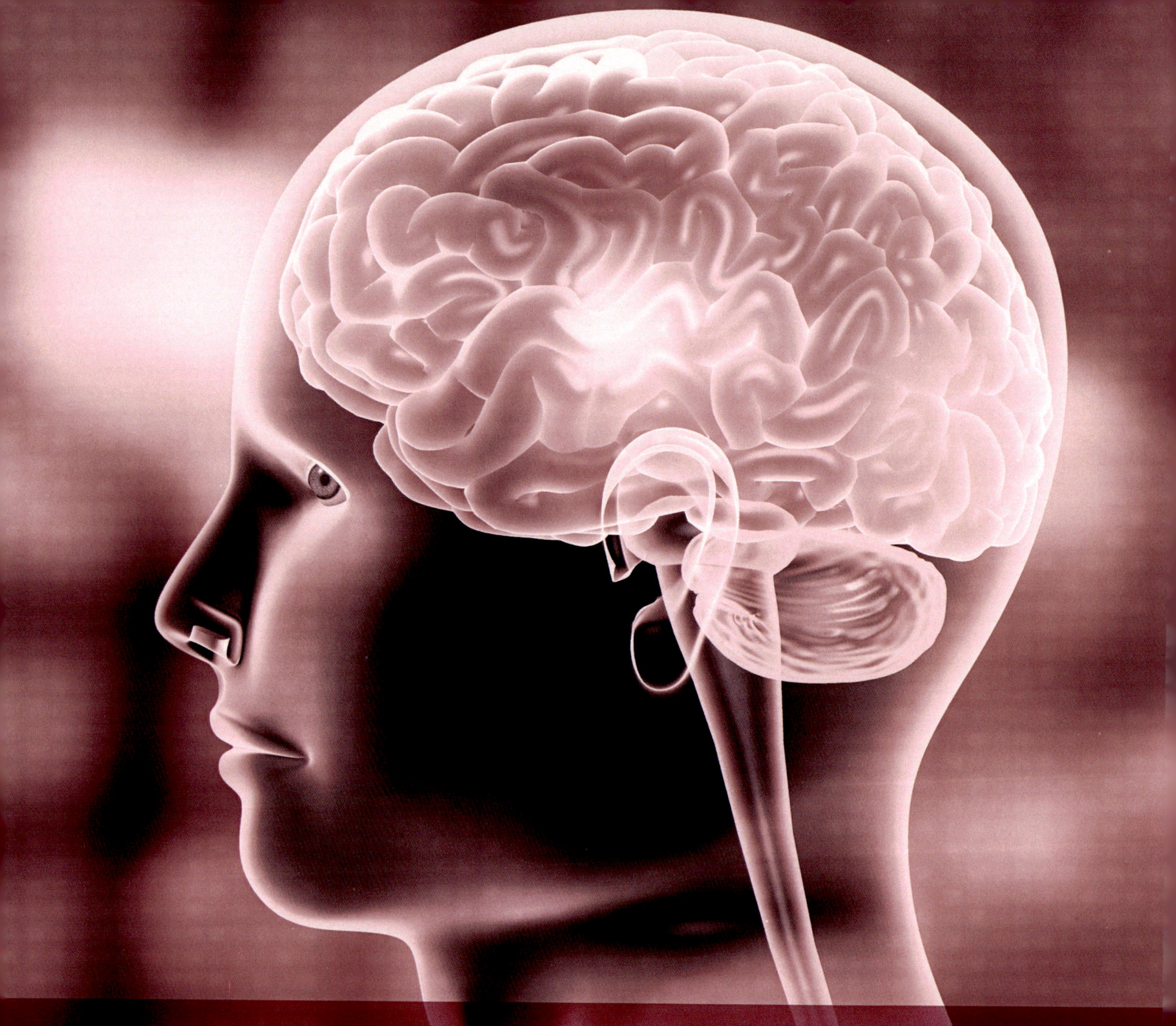

Chapter 8: Prevention

People who have one concussion are at a higher risk for being injured with another concussion in the future. Unfortunately, the long-term effects of concussions grow with every injury. Athletes should take steps to prevent concussions before they happen.

Culture

The single best way to prevent concussions is to create an environment where you aren't hit in the head. This may mean delaying contact sports until you're older. Making sure that you know proper technique for tackling can also help keep your brain safe.

It's also important to have a sports culture where head injuries are taken seriously. When an athlete shows signs of a concussion, coaches and teammates need to make sure the athlete receives treatment. Taking that athlete out of play is the most significant step in preventing further injury.

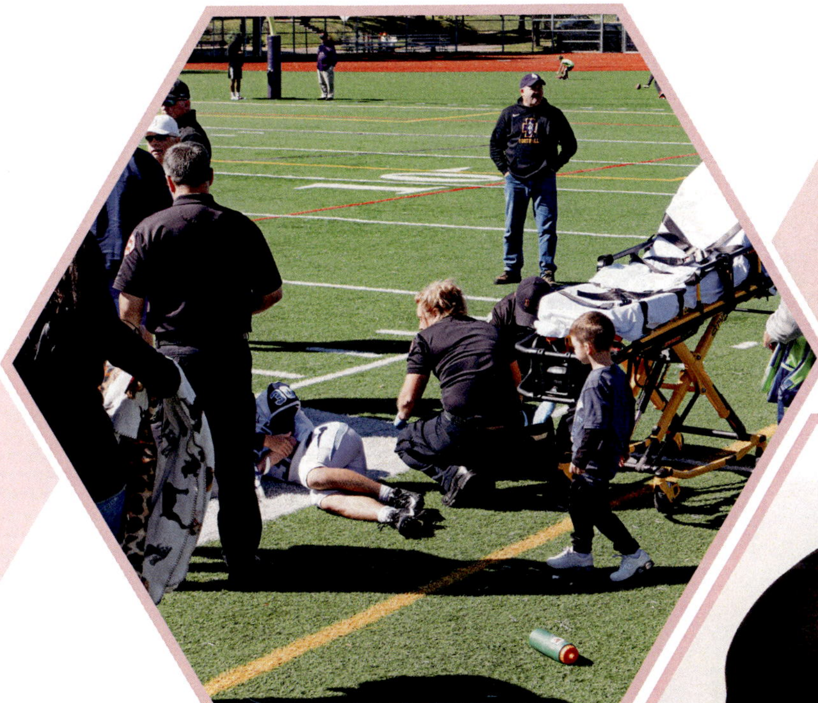

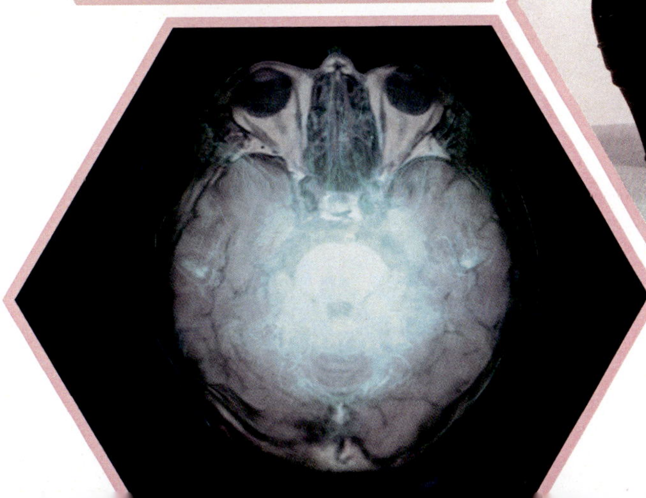

Equipment

Equipment such as helmets, mouthguards, and pads may help protect your body, but they will not prevent concussions. To prevent injuries such as skull fractures, you should wear up-to-date helmets and pads. Engineers and scientists are working to develop equipment that will prevent concussions, but so far, the only way to avoid a concussion is to not be hit in the head.

Scientists can use mouthguards to study concussions. They put accelerometers, or sensors that detect changes in speed, in the mouthguards to help them understand how players have been hit.

A concussion is a common sports injury. Though symptoms of a concussion may be scary, most athletes will recover with rest and time away from the sport. While wearing proper safety equipment will help keep you safe from other injuries, there is no equipment that will prevent concussions. It's important to pay attention to symptoms of concussions and make sure you have plenty of rest after a concussion in order to prevent additional injury.

Glossary

anatomy (un-NAT-uh-mee): The study of the parts of the human body

arachnoid (uh-RAK-noid): The middle of three layers protecting the brain

bone (bohn): A hard material in the human body that provides structure

cell (sel): The basic unit of all living things

cerebrospinal fluid (suh-ree-broh-SPAHYN-l FLOO-id): A cushion between the arachnoid and pia matter

chronic traumatic encephalopathy (KRON-ik truh-MAT-ik en-sef-uh-LOP-uh-thee): A severe brain injury, likely caused by too many hits to the head

cranial bone (KREY-nee-uhl bohn): One of eight bones that make up the human skull

dura matter (DOOR-uh MEY-ter): The outer-most of three layers protecting the human brain

heading (HED-ing): Bouncing a ball off the head

joint/s (joint): Where two or more bones meet

meninges (mi-NIN-jeez): The three layers of protective covering of the human brain

motor skill (MOH-ter skil): Using specific motions to accomplish a task

magnetic resonance imaging (mag-NET-ik REZ-uh-nuhns IM-uh-jing): A machine that uses magnets to take images of the soft parts inside the human body, commonly known as MRI

pia matter (PEE-uh MAT-er): The inner-most of three layers protecting the human brain

skull (skuhl): The bone of the head

spinal cord (SPAHYN-l kawrd): Nerve tissue running from the brain through the spinal column

tissue (TIS-yoo): A group of cells that perform a specific function

traumatic (truh-MAT-ik): A wound created by a sudden shock

X-ray (EKS-rey): Electromagnetic radiation with a shorter wavelength than light that can show images of hard tissue like bone

vertigo (VUR-ti-goh): Being dizzy or feeling unstable while in fact on firm ground

whiplash (HWIP-lash): A head and neck injury where the head is suddenly jerked forward or backward, rotating on the neck

Index

Comprehension Questions

1. Which of these can give an athlete a concussion?
    a. Drinking too much water
    b. Not stretching enough
    c. Heading a soccer ball
2. True or false: any sport where a player's head is hit has a risk of concussion
3. How many layers are there to the meninges?
    a. 2
    b. 3
    c. 5
4. True or false: the most important aspect of recovering from a concussion is rest.
5. True or false: athletes can have as much screen time as they want while recovering from a concussion
6. One example of a balance test is
    a. Standing on one foot
    b. Reading words off of a card
    c. Laying down on an exam table
7. When an athlete feels dizzy after being hit in the head they should
    a. Stop playing and tell their coach
    b. Close their eyes and count to 10
    c. Eat a snack
8. True or false: mouthguards help prevent concussions

1. c 2. true 3. b 4. true 5. false 6. a 7. a 8. false

About the Author

India James writes about science, technology, and math for young readers. She loves when science comes together with sports. India lives in Ohio with her family.

Author: India James

Editor: Ellen Rodger

Design: Jen Bowers

IMAGE CREDITS

Shutterstock: Cover and title page ©2022 Mahir KART (p.4), ©2019 CGN089 (p.14), ©2016 Margaret Kite (p.5), ©2016 Rocketclips, Inc. (p.24); p.4 ©2019 Alex Kravtsov; p.5 ©2019 Explode (p.40); p.6 ©2020 Paul Yates, ©2021 Fabrizio Andrea Bertani; p.7 ©2021 Pixel-Shot; p.8 ©2019 Orla, ©2023 Jo Panuwat D; p.9 ©2019 Golden Shrimp (p.18), ©Natata; p.10 ©2024 Creative Elegant, ©VectorMine; p.11 ©2016 stihii, ©2022 PeopleImages.com - Yuri A; p.12 ©VectorMine; p.13 ©Alexander_P; p.14 ©2020 Radiological imaging (p.41); p.15 ©Pepermpron; p.16 ©2022 PeopleImages.com - Yuri A; p.17 ©2024 Andrey_Popov; p.18 ©2024 Yurii_Yarema, ©2024 PanuShot; p.19 ©2020 Prostock-studio, ©2023 Prostock-studio, © 2017 Kleber Cordeiro; p.20 ©2024 PeopleImages.com - Yuri A; p.21 ©2021 Pixel-Shot; p.22 ©Pepermpron; p.23 ©2024 NassornSnitwong; p.24 ©2016 Rocketclips, Inc.; p.25 ©2022 Master1305; p.27 ©2024 A.RICARDO, ©2023 Pierre Teyssot; p.28 ©2021 fizkes, ©2016 Ground Picture; p.29 ©2021 Microgen; p.30 ©2019 Andrey_Popov; p.31 ©2023 anek.soowannaphoom; p.32 ©2024 Pixel-Shot, ©2022 Media Lens King; p.33 ©2024 meeboonstudio; p.34 ©2024 PeopleImages.com - Yuri A, ©2023 Jacob Lund; p.35 ©2024 Pixel-Shot; p.36 ©2024 Prostock-studio; p.37 ©2019 Rocketclips, Inc.; p.38 ©2024 Lightspring; p.39 ©2024 PeopleImages.com - Yuri A; p.40 ©2022 Ringo Chiu; p.41 ©2020 Steve Skjold, ©2017 Bobby Stevens Photo; p.42 ©2024 Solomon Thompson, ©2014 Mega Pixel; p.43 ©2022 Prostock-studio; p.48 About the Author image ©Alvesgaspar

Crabtree Publishing

crabtreebooks.com 800-387-7650

In Canada: We acknowledge the financial support of the Government of Canada through the Canada Book Fund for our publishing activities.

Hardcover 978-1-0398-8080-1
Paperback 978-1-0398-8441-0
Ebook (pdf) 978-1-0398-8200-3
Epub 978-1-0398-8320-8

Published in Canada
Crabtree Publishing
616 Welland Avenue
St. Catharines, Ontario
L2M 5V6

Published in the United States
Crabtree Publishing
347 Fifth Avenue
Suite 1402-145
New York, New York, 10016

Library and Archives Canada Cataloguing in Publication
Available at Library and Archives Canada

Library of Congress Cataloging-in-Publication Data
Available at the Library of Congress

Printed in the USA/CP2025